W9-AVB-084

Postcard Quilts

GIFTS TO MAKE AND MAIL

by Caroline Reardon

Edited by Maria Reardon Capp
Book design and additional artwork
by Annie Segal

PRIMEDIA Consumer Media & Magazine Group
741 Corporate Circle, Golden, CO 80401

Table of Contents

Additional copies are available for purchase for U.S. $19.95.
Please call 1-800-590-3465 within USA. Outside USA, phone 720-836-1123 or 800-590-3465.

Order online at www.villagequiltshoppe.com

Copyright © 2005 by **PRIMEDIA** Consumer Media & Magazine Group
741 Corporate Circle, Golden, CO 80401

All rights reserved. No part of this book may be reproduced in any form or by any means without the prior written permission of the publisher, excepting copies made to adjust patterns for personal use only.

First Printing 2005
Manufactured in Korea
ISBN:0-9770414-0-9

Shortly after retiring as the editor of *Quiltmaker* in June 2004, I started making quilted fabric postcards, first as little thank you's for retirement gifts and then for family and friends' birthdays. I love the instant gratification — fun to design, quick to make, and rewarding to give. Everyone's excited to get these little quilts in the mail, sent just like a regular postcard — no envelope — but with hand canceling. Some people have suggested that I make them to sell, but I'd rather produce the patterns for you to create your own. So here I am, back to the pattern-publishing business!

These postcards consist of three layers: a picture, a stiff interfacing and a backing for the addresses and message, with an optional inner layer of muslin. Because many of the patches in this 4$\frac{1}{2}$" x 6$\frac{1}{2}$" format are very small, they are fused in place using a quick and easy process. You can choose to just fuse, or you can fuse and then machine quilt any of the postcard projects. Add a traditional binding or finish quickly with a fused one.

Throughout the book, you'll find patterns and alternatives that fit your working style, design preferences and time constraints. Some are simple (Fisherman's Birthday, page 26) and some much more detailed (Whimsy Garden, page 68). You can make a pattern template to ensure exact patch placement or you can take the casual approach. Choose from optional shapes to customize your picture, compose your own words from alphabets given, borrow a design from one pattern to use in another. Draw lines with a fabric pen or stitch them in contrasting thread. Those who love scrapbooking can convert these designs to paper and glue them to mat board for mailing. So many choices!

Whichever designs, techniques and materials you use, I hope you find here the inspiration to create and mail postcard quilts to the special people in your life. You'll have as much fun making them as they will have getting them in the mail.

Caroline

Things You Need

Assorted Fabric Scraps

The more fabrics in your stash, the happier you'll be when making postcards. Obviously you won't need much of any one piece (4½" x 6½" is the largest) but it's nice to have lots of options for the yummy pink frosting or distant purple mountain or white stork feathers or… Good quality cotton gives excellent results, but also consider lamé and other specialty fabrics for special effects. I love to use batik fabrics because the tight weave resists fraying and the complete dye penetration ensures color at the cut edges.

Fusible Webbing

If you choose to just fuse, use a no-sew fusible web like HeatnBond® Ultra Hold to ensure a strong bond of the fabric layers. If you plan to machine quilt the piece after fusing, use a light fusible web such as HeatnBond® Lite so the needle will stitch through the patches easily.

Pressing Sheet

A nonstick pressing sheet, such as The Applique Pressing Sheet™ by Bear Thread Designs, is a great help in building units within some designs (see page 31). It also protects your ironing board from fusible web. A piece of backing paper that has been peeled away from just-fused fabric also makes a good pressing sheet.

Stiffener

A stiff white needlepunched polyester interfacing gives the postcard the firmness needed for mailing. Look for 23"-wide Timtex Interfacing™ or 22"-wide Pellon® Peltex® at large fabric stores. One-eighth yard will make three postcards. If you have trouble finding this thick interfacing, substitute artist's canvas or three layers of garment interfacing.

Tracing Paper

Quilter's or artist's tracing paper comes in tablet form or on a roll. You'll find it at many quilt shops and art and office supply stores.

Adhesive Spray

Machine-embroidery adhesive spray, such as that made by Sullivans, holds the tissue-paper pattern in place on the fabric for cutting. It also holds the layers of fabric and stiffener together during construction. You'll be so glad you have this!

Permanent-Ink Pens

For lettering, The Gelly Roll medium pen by Sakura is my favorite; the ink does not bleed. For shading with tiny dots and lines, Sakura's Pigma Micron 01 and 03 pens are good.

Additional Supplies for Quilting the Postcards

Thread

Most of the postcards in this book are machine quilted with clear monofilament thread in the top of the sewing machine and white thread in the bobbin. Overall dark designs *(Close to the Forest,* page 86) are best quilted with smoky monofilament thread and dark bobbin thread. For thread work in a design *(Waiting Room,* page 52), the slender #60 machine-embroidery thread works well.

Needles

I like to use the thinnest machine needle available, size #60/8, because it makes the smallest hole through the many layers. Do be careful when free-motion quilting, though, because these needles break a bit more easily. A larger needle is fine; you'll just have larger holes.

Things You'll Be Glad You Have

6½" x 6½" Acrylic Ruler

If you plan to make many post-cards, you'll love the convenience of this little ruler with a width exactly postcard size.

Waxed Paper

To keep track of and to store adhesive-backed traced-paper patterns. Because I lose these little pieces so easily, this has become a required element in my system.

Freezer Paper

To stabilize the backing while writing the addresses and message.

Old Newspaper

A great backdrop when spraying the adhesive. Spread out several sheets to protect surfaces from the fan of the spray.

Embellishments

Relatively flat decorations like glitter fabric paint and puff paint in tubes, sequins, seed beads, metallic thread, rickrack, lace, ribbon and buttons add a little glitz.

Glue

My favorite glue for adhering embellishments is E6000® by Eclectic Products. Look for it at fabric, office supply and craft stores.

Making the Postcard

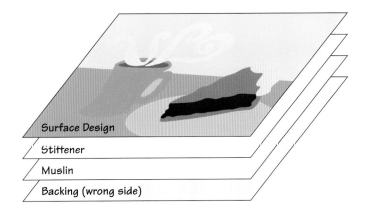

Surface Design

Stiffener

Muslin

Backing (wrong side)

Cutting

Background fabric: 1 @ 4½" x 6½"

Assorted scraps

Stiffener: 1 @ 4½" x 6½"

Muslin: 1 @ 4½" x 6½" (Not needed for fused-only postcards)

Backing (address side): 1 @ 4½" x 6½"

Binding fabric: 1 @ 1" x 23"
(For fused-only binding: 1 @ 3" x 7", which later will be cut into strips)

Directions

The patterns are given as they appear in finished form; the easy process described here does not use reversed images for the fusing process.

Read the tips on pattern pages throughout the book before you begin. Many of them apply to all the designs, and you'll be glad for the information when you start your project.

Study your chosen design to determine the order for fusing from background to front. Some postcards will have specific construction suggestions if details differ from the general instructions.

Making Templates

Cut two pieces of tracing paper, each 5" x 7".

On one, trace all the lines of the postcard pattern you've chosen. This Pattern Template will be your guide when positioning patches for fusing. If you're the improvising type and want to position the pieces more casually, you won't need this Template.

On the other piece of paper, trace the lines of the address pattern given on the next page to make the Address Template. Include the cake design only if you'll include it on your postcard. Improvisers may choose to omit this too.

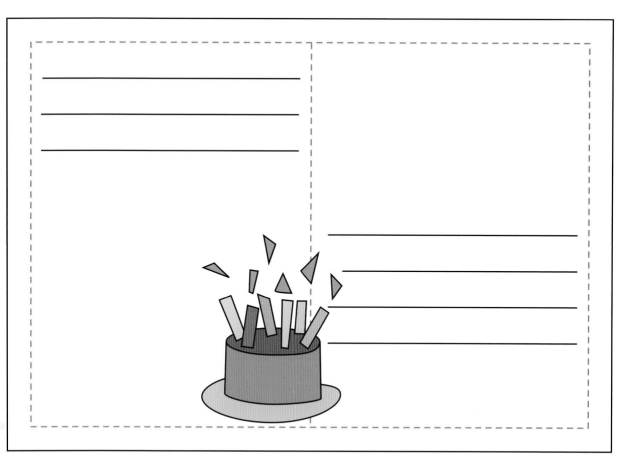

Creating Patch Patterns

On tracing paper, trace each patch outline, leaving a little space between images. For a patch that lies partially under another, extend its line approximately ⅛" (for example, the top crust of the pie in *Pie & Coffee,* page 62), or complete its shape (the plate under the pie).

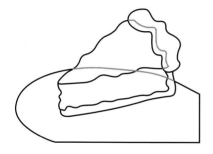

Place the traced paper face down on sheets of old newspaper. (I spread newspaper out on the floor in my sewing room away from traffic, but then I don't have a a toddler or a dog in the house…) Lightly spray the wrong side of the paper. Cut the patterns apart and place sticky side down on waxed paper.

Cutting the Patches

Look through your fabric stash to find the colors and prints for your chosen design, starting with the background fabric and then auditioning fabric for each of the patches against this one.

For each fabric cut a piece of fusible web at least as large as the patch you'll need. If you plan to make several postcards, consider backing larger pieces of fabric with the webbing. I love having a stash of fuse-backed fabrics ready to cut.

Following the manufacturer's directions, fuse the webbing to the wrong side of the fabric. Remove the paper.

Press the traced pattern exactly where you want it, adhesive-side down, on the right side of the fuse-backed fabric. Cut on the drawn line. Remove the pattern and put it back on the waxed paper.

If any patch needs inked lines or features, position it over the pattern and trace them now.

Making and Tracing a Word Template

To trace lettering on the background (*The Home Stretch,* page 54) or patches (*Animal Parade,* page 56), first make a Word Template: On tracing paper, draw a base line and trace the letters you need along the line. Then tape the Template on a light table or sunny window.

Position the patch over the Template and tape this in place too. Trace the letters.

Fusing the Design

Place the background fabric on the stiffener; it will make a good "platform" to transport all the pieces to the ironing board later. Arrange the patches on the background in approximate position. If you're questioning any fabric choices, recut those patches now from fabrics you like better.

Take the stiffener with background and patches to your ironing board. Center the Pattern Template over the background and hold it in place along one edge. Using it as a guide, move the patches into position under the template. I find a long straight pin is helpful here.

Remove the Template and carefully fuse the patches down with a hot, dry iron. You may want to cover the work with the pressing sheet before fusing. For some designs, fusing partial areas at a time works best; these are described in the particular patterns. Follow the suggested time for pressing; less is better than more.

Spray the wrong side of the fused background and one side of the stiffener with the adhesive spray. Aligning edges, press the sprayed sides together.

If you have used no-sew fusible webbing, you are ready to make the address side of the postcard. Skip to that section now.

Machine Quilting

As you will see, a few of the postcard designs are enhanced by thread work (*Waiting Room,* page 52), which also serves as the quilting, while others have minimal quilting with monofilament thread (*Playmates,* page 72). I wanted to show you both; you can decide how much, if any, thread work to do. If you like a more textural look, add quilting to the background as well. Compare *Bouquets* on pages 66 and 92 for these treatments.

If you're using monofilament thread, remember to loosen the upper tension of your sewing machine. For free-motion quilting, use a darning foot and disengage the feed dogs. For straight or slightly curved quilting lines, I like to use an open-toe embroidery foot and keep feed dogs up – I can see where I'm going and the stitches are nice and even.

Before machine quilting the postcard, it's best to practice on a test piece made from layering two pieces of fabric over the stiffener. I do this so I can make sure the machine tension is good and that I've remembered to install the #60/8 needle.

Take a look at the suggested quilting for the photographed postcard and then decide what you'd like to do. Catching every patch in the quilting is the primary goal, so a very simple quilting plan may be enough. If you need to stop or start in the center of the piece, sew three stitches in place, and then when quilting is complete, cut the thread tails close to the surface.

This is a good time to sew on any dimensional embellishments. Place them no closer than ½" from the edge so the presser foot will have an "open road" when sewing the binding.

Addressing the Backing

Choose a light colored fabric that complements the design and style of the postcard picture. If you use a print, make sure that it is plain enough for the lettering to be legible. Sometimes the wrong side of a fabric is perfect for the backing's subtle hue.

To stabilize the backing: Cut a piece of freezer paper 4½" x 6½" and center it shiny side down on the wrong side of the backing. With a hot, dry iron press the layers together.

If you want word guides: On the Address Template you made earlier, trace the letters from an alphabet on the next page to make addresses and messages. Then tape this Template on a light box or sunny window. Tape the backing right side up over the Template and trace the words with a permanent-ink pen.

If you want just line guides: Tape the Address Template on a light box or sunny window. Tape the backing right side up over the Template. Using the lines as a guide, write the addresses with a permanent-ink pen and then add your message.

Or, write addresses and messages free-hand.

Peel away the freezer paper. With spray adhesive, adhere the wrong side of the backing to the muslin. (The muslin makes the backing look smoother over the quilting and hides any dark bobbin threads. You can omit this layer if you want.) Fold this layered piece in half and crease to create a vertical line down the center. Open and stitch the layers together along this crease.

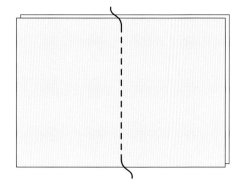

If you are fusing patches to the backing, such as the small birthday cake, do that now. Use no-sew fusible web for these patches or machine quilt just enough to hold them in place.

Spray the wrong sides of the front and backing surfaces with adhesive. Aligning edges, press them together. Using an acrylic ruler and rotary cutter, trim to get straight edges and square corners.

Finishing

All these postcards have fabric bindings that were applied with one of three techniques: Machine/ Hand, Machine/Machine or Fused. I've used the Machine/Hand method most often because it makes a beautiful finish, and I like doing handwork while watching TV in the evening. The Machine/ Machine binding *(Love, Love, Love, page 38)* is quicker and works well if you are careful with measuring. The Fused binding *(Fisherman's Birthday, page 26)* is perfect for the no-sew postcard.

A B C D E F G H I J K L M
N O P Q R S T U V W X Y Z
a b c d e f g h i j k l m n o p q r s t u v w x y z
1 2 3 4 5 6 7 8 9 0 . , ! ? " " ' '

A B C D E F G H I J K L M
N O P Q R S T U V W X Y Z
A B C D E F G H I J K L M N
O P Q R S T U V W X Y Z . , ! ?
a b c d e f g h i j k l m n
o p q r s t u v w x y z
1 2 3 4 5 6 7 8 9 0 " " ' '

Machine/Hand Binding

1. Fold one short edge of the binding strip 90° to the wrong side and press. Trim ¼" from the fold. Turn in the adjacent long edge a **scant** ¼" and press.

2. Aligning raw edges, lay the binding strip right side down on the right side of the postcard. Begin sewing at the folded end with a **scant** ¼" seam allowance. Stop ¼" from the first corner, backstitch, remove the postcard from the machine and cut the threads.

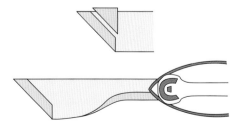

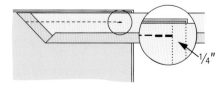

¼"

Fold the binding up, then back down even with the edge of the postcard. Begin stitching at the edge of the next side, backstitch and continue sewing. Repeat the process at each corner.

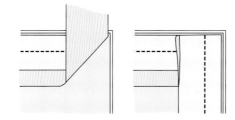

When you reach the beginning fold, overlap the end of the strip and stitch ½" beyond the fold underneath. Trim the tail parallel to the fold.

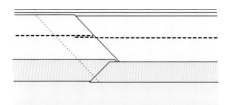

3. Turn the binding to the back and blind stitch it to the backing by hand, covering the previous line of stitches. Fold the corners as shown and blind stitch.

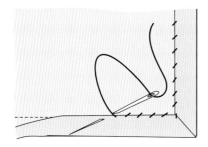

Machine/Machine Binding

With this method, final stitching shows on the front. I like to use a programmed wavy stitch so I don't have to worry about straight stitching exactly along the edge. Before beginning, test stitch widths and lengths until you get the one you like.

1. Follow step 1 in Machine/Hand binding.

2. Sew the binding strip to the backing rather than to the front, following step 2 of the Machine/Hand binding technique.

3. Turn the binding to the front. Gently pull the folded edge over the previous stitching as you sew it down by machine, folding each corner in the direction you're sewing and pin in place before you get to it.

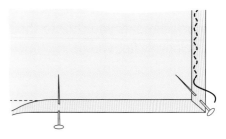

Fused Binding

Fuse the wrong side of a 3" x 7" piece of fabric with no-sew webbing and remove the paper. From this fabric, cut 4 strips ¾" x 7".

On the ironing board, place one strip right side down. Center a short side of the postcard right side up halfway in along this strip. Fold over the remaining half of the strip to the front, making the strip snug against the stiffener along the edge. Fuse in place and leave the postcard undisturbed for a few seconds. Turn the card to the back and fuse down the other half. Let it cool and then trim the extra lengths. Repeat for the opposite side. Follow the same process to fuse the top and bottom binding strips.

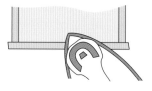

Embellishing
Most of the postcards in this book are not embellished; I wanted the designs to "stand on their own," but many are good candidates for glitter paint, beads, sequins, braiding or other trims. Remember that the embellishments you choose should be relatively flat; you never know how much friction the postcard will be subjected to in the mail. And plan ahead because paints and glues need time to dry before the postcard is mailed.

Ring for Hanging
If your recipient might want to hang the postcard art, hand sew a little ring at the top center of the backing. I use a 6mm or 9mm jewelry jump ring, available at many craft and fabric stores. Sew securely at the base of the ring, only through the backing layer. Knot the thread and pop the knot through the fabric as you would do when ending a line of hand quilting. Then just tack the sides with a stitch or two. When your friend calls to thank you for such a unique gift, explain that the side threads can be snipped to free the ring for a hanger.

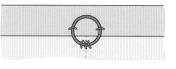

Mailing
A postcard made with this technique needs 49¢ postage because of its thickness. At the time of this writing, that means a 48¢ stamp and a 1¢ stamp. I like the tidiness of one stamp, so have often chosen to send my cards with one 60¢ stamp instead. Just to be safe, I adhere the stamp with a little extra glue. And I personally deliver my postcard to the post office and watch it being hand canceled. The post office clerks have as much fun seeing them as I have making them so it's a nice send off.

And now to the designs. You might want to start with a very simple one like *Close to the Forest,* page 86, to work through the process, but if you're ready to send a birthday gift, *Happy Birthday* on the next page is a great beginning. Have fun!

Happy Birthday!

The first birthday postcard I made was for Sophie, our oldest grand-daughter. Hers had nine candles and some of the swirls turned into the numeral 9. Creating it was such fun and she was amazed that this unusual gift came "unwrapped" through the mail. Since then I've made birthday postcards for family and friends, varying fabric combinations, shapes of swirls, stars, candles and confetti. I always look forward to making the next one.

Start with a festive but subtle print for the background and then find two contrasting frosting colors that look good on the background. The plate fabric should be darker than the cake. Snip off triangle-shaped flames from

strips of yellow, gold and orange. I like the confetti (not patterned) to look rectangular. See the tip on page 69 to create a stash of snippets good for cutting candles, flames and confetti.

With clear monofilament thread, outline quilt patches of the cake and plate; then free-motion quilt the background, catching all the little patches at least once in the stitching.

If you like, decorate with puff paint, glitter paint or sequins, and sew seed beads on top of the cake for "sprinkles."

Happy Chapeau

Rather than using the traditional cake motif, make and send this post-card to your wild and crazy friend as a fun and unique gift for her birthday. Notice that the candle flames are more shapely than those on the cake – a bit more feminine for the red hot mamma!

Audition your main hat fabric on the darker background to make sure it shows up well, and then look for a darker shade for the underbrim. After all patches are fused in place, you might like to add a metallic braid for added sparkle. If sequins, rhinestones or glitter are your choice, wait until the postcard has been quilted before gluing these in place.

To celebrate another occasion, change the birthday chapeau to a spring bonnet with this band of flowers, motifs borrowed from *Bouquet,* page 66.

Make a Wish

The day our granddaughter Emmaline was born, cousin Benjamin gave her a stuffed toy named Pegasus. For Emma's second birthday, I made this card for her and her constant companion, since they share this special day.

If you don't have rainbow fabric for the wings, color white fabric with crayons, cover with paper and heat set with an iron. Add a pupil to the eye patch with black ink and then hand stitch a dot of white thread for sparkle in its eye.

Free-motion thread work that embellishes the mane and tail also quilts those areas. I used metallic thread to quilt the wings and monofilament thread for everything else.

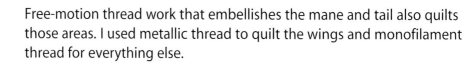

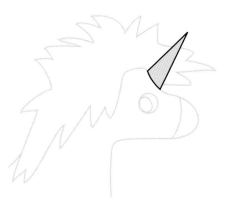

After the postcard was bound, I added metallic stars on the cake and pearlized puff paint for Peg's breath blowing out the candles.

If your little one would rather have a unicorn, add a horn to its forehead.

Birthday for a Princess

For your favorite little girl who loves the story "The Princess and the Pea" by Hans Christian Anderson, send this little quilt as a birthday surprise. Since the bed with all the comforters fills this side, add a birthday cake to the backing. See page 7.

This stack includes 17 fabrics for comforters and one for the pillow. Use one of the darkest shades behind the pea to make it obvious. Don't worry if your stack is not just like this one; cut wavy edges and rounded ends for a soft, cozy look. Separately construct the princess and the stack of comforters with unit fusing as explained on page 31. After the floor has

been fused to the background, drape some of the bottom comforter over the bed frame before fusing all in place.

I defined the bed frame and some areas of the princess with little dots and lines from fine-line permanent ink pens, using brown ink for softer shadowing and black for sharper edges.

Outline quilt the patches with monofilament thread.

Star Party

This design, appropriate for any age, may appeal especially to teenagers who identify with the cheering party scene.

First cut out the silhouettes from the black fabric. Then audition these on blue background candidates to find the best contrast. Following the tip on page 31, build the star-trail unit. Place this over the letters in the pattern and/ or on page 11 and ink in your message before fusing it to the background.

To outline quilt the silhouettes, use dark thread in the bobbin and smoky monofilament thread in the top. Change to light bobbin thread and clear monofilament to quilt wavy lines in the stars and trail.

Substitute this landscape silhouette if it's more appropriate for your message.

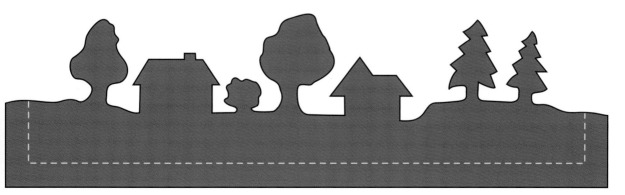

Happy Hold 'em

Do you know someone who loves playing poker – Friday-night-with-the-guys games, internet games, family-get-together games? If so, use this design that I created for my husband, Michael.

Collect a variety of reds, blues and whites for the chips and add fusible webbing to the wrong side of small pieces of each. Notice that the blue chips are the largest, the whites are smallest. Don't worry about following the pattern for individual chips; just cut shallow ovals in each of the three sizes and trim the ends flat. You'll find this design much easier to construct if you build the stacks with unit fusing as explained on page 31. Make confetti, not shown in the pattern, by cutting snippets from fuse-backed strips.

Quilt along the edges of the chips and card patches and then free-motion quilt in loops over the background, stitching at least once through each confetti piece and along the swirls.

The postcard needed a little more sparkle, so after it was quilted I glued stars on the flames and brushed touches of glitter paint on the green table.

For "Happy Retirement," you could send this card without the candles to someone who now has time for favorite activities!

Fisherman's Birthday

Your fisherman friend will enjoy this simple image of a fish; it may remind him of his best catch mounted on a plaque. If you want a bit more whimsy, give the swimmer a party hat!

I was lucky to find this scale print in my stash. Wiggly stripes and plaids would also work well for a semi-natural look, or go crazy and make him in bright bold geometrics. My medium-value fish on dark purple needed an outline of black permanent ink to help it stand out from the background.

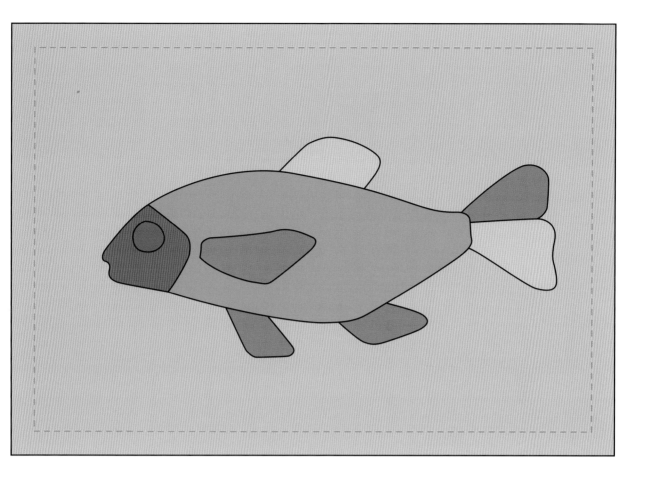

This postcard has no stitching; the entire piece has been fused with no-sew fusible web – including the binding. It is, of course, the fastest of the processes given in the book, and it has a clean and direct presentation.

If you want to add quilting, be sure to start with the lightweight fusible web for the bonding. Irregular, horizontal wavy lines quilted across the piece would be appealing as would swirly whirls.

Invite a Dragon

One day our grandson Benjamin said his favorite animal was a dragon. That's all I needed to get started on the postcard for his sixth birthday.

I auditioned lots of "reptilian-print" batiks and settled on the main body fabric because it looks kind of friendly. Then I added more subtle prints for the wing, back, legs and spine scales. This big guy was just going to be a guest at the party until I realized he could help by lighting the candles with his fiery breath.

Ben's postcard is more personalized because he's wearing his favorite green shirt and purposely mismatched socks.

Because of his size, the dragon wraps around to the address side with his tail finally appearing under the stamp area. If the background fabric for the front is too busy for words to be legible on this side, choose a fabric in a similar color to keep the same look.

Following the tip on the facing page, fuse the boy and the cake as units.

Rather than cutting individual triangles for the back scales, cut a strip of fabric 1" x 8" and then cut zigzags through the center, leaving a ⅛"-wide margin on both long sides to tuck under the body before fusing.

With monofilament thread outline quilt the patches and stipple quilt the dragon's body. Quilt the wing and foot as shown by the dashed lines.

After binding, I glued a 7mm emerald green rhinestone in place for the dragon's eye. A sequin or glitter paint also would work well here.

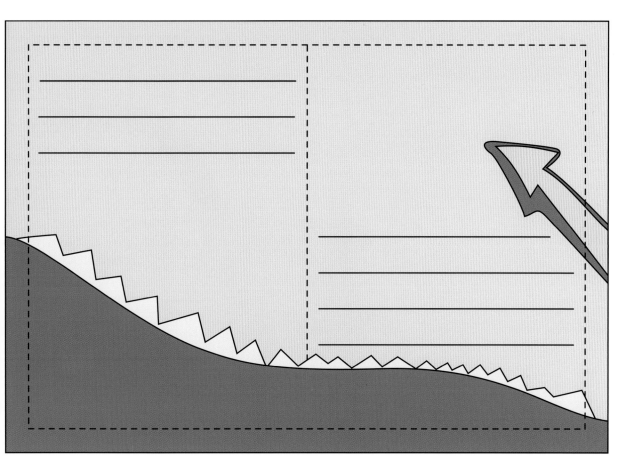

Fusing Units

Some images have such small pieces that they are difficult to position and fuse on the background at the same time you are fusing surrounding patches. If you first build these detailed figures as independent units, they are much easier to handle when composing the entire picture.

Take your Patch Template, the fuse-backed patches and the nonstick pressing sheet to the ironing board. Starting with the patch lowest in the layering, position one or two patches in place on the sheet and lightly fuse them together. Continue building from the bottom up, lightly fusing as you go. Avoid overheating; the fabric may absorb the webbing and make it ineffective. Let the unit cool and then peel it off the sheet.

Takin' the Cake

Grandson Antonio has always loved trucks, so naturally a truck had to be on his birthday postcard. He also loves hitches on trucks, and while he rides in Grandad's truck, they both count the mounted hitches they pass on the streets. And now our youngest grandson, Ethan, is talking trucks, so a similar postcard for his second birthday is in the making.

This birthday postcard features a candle in the shape of a number on top of the cake. Since it's white, face it following the tip on page 39. If you have a little bit of silver lamé, back it with fusible interfacing and then fusible webbing; cut the hubcaps, bumper and hitch patches from this fabric.

Find a background fabric that looks like sky and another in a different shade that reminds you of glass reflecting sky. The fabric used for the window was the background of a fish print that I'd wondered why I kept after cleaning out my stash several months ago. You just never know when you'll need that "odd" piece!

After cutting out the cab of the truck, position it over the Pattern Template and, following the horizontal lines, write the address with permanent ink. If you first want to check spacing, make a Word Template, tracing letters from the alphabet on page 11 before writing on the patch. Then fuse all in place, starting with the black fabric behind the wheel.

Outline quilt around the truck, trailer and cake shapes and zigzag quilt the number outline, all in monofilament thread. Stitch a little swirly pattern in the hubcaps. To add more interest, change to green thread in the top and quilt grass behind the trailer.

Sew colorful seed beads (or glue sequins) to the cake after all the quilting is done to make the picture more festive.

Valentine Tree

The *Valentine Tree* has a folk-art look with fresh colors of spring. When selecting fabrics, choose a subtle color for the tree trunk and branches patch; the hearts and birds should be the focus of attention.

After I had fused everything in place, I felt that the bird on the left was not dark enough so I added more blue with a crayon. Read more about this trick on page 49 – it's one of my favorites!

Striped fabric cut perpendicular to the bands makes a festive binding.

With monofilament thread, I quilted loops over the surface of this design, making sure to stitch over every patch to hold it down.

In addition to using this design for Valentine's Day, it would be perfect to send your "Congratulations" for an engagement, wedding or anniversary.

Another idea: At the base of the tree add the little bird from *A Little Bird Told Me* on page 50 and send the postcard as a gift to the new parents.

Love, Love, Love

Put a contemporary twist to your valentine card by using brights with black and white prints. This combination is a great choice when you're not sending a romantic message, just a happy note to a dear friend.

If you fuse light fabric over a black and white print, the black images will probably show through. To avoid this, face the light fabric, following the tip on the next page.

Free-motion quilt around the hearts and make smaller heart shapes inside. Stitch along the edges of the other shapes as well.

Notice the binding on this one; it is the machine/machine technique described on page 12. The wavy final stitching on the binding adds a decorative element to the edging – and it finishes faster than the machine/hand method.

See page 61 for more heart shapes.

Faced for Fusing

If you will be fusing a light-colored patch over a dark patch or dark motif in a print, the dark outline may show through from underneath. To avoid this, first fuse white fabric to the wrong side of the light fabric. Then add webbing to the wrong side of the white one. Treat this sandwich as one when cutting and fusing the patch.

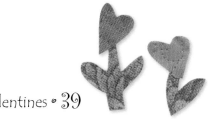

Luv Ya!

Luscious lips send your valentine a message in big bold letters for all the world to see – or at least his mail carrier!

The white balloon will be fused over both the black and the red with the real possibility of those colors showing through. To keep the white bright, first face it as explained in the tip on page 39.

Then trace this message here or another given on page 61. If you would rather compose your own, first make a Word Template as explained on page 8 before tracing from the alphabet on page 61.

Fuse and quilt the lips before adding the balloon. This way, you can quilt the lips in a continuous line. Since the curves are gradual, you can keep the feed dogs up and use the regular presser foot; this will regulate the stitch length and make an attractive quilting line. I used red bobbin thread with monofilament in the top for the lips and changed to white bobbin thread for the balloon, just in case my machine tension wasn't perfect.

After the postcard is finished, add a light film of glitter paint to the lips if you like.

Congrats!

Doesn't this design remind you of a stage with dancing letters? In browns, blacks and rusts, it seems happy but not frilly – perfect for a guy. For a more lighthearted look, go with lighter, brighter colors.

If you have plenty of the fabric you'll use behind the letters, cut it 4½" x 6½" for the background. If not, cut a piece of muslin this size and then fuse all the patches to it.

More words and an alphabet are given on page 47. If you want a longer word, extend the center patch and make the side angled patches narrower. Try placing the letters in a straight line and then bouncing them around

Try placing the letters in a straight line and then bouncing them around to see which you like better. You can fit more letters if they bounce. And notice that I didn't cut out the centers of letters "A" and "R." They're just too small and it's easy to tell what the letters are just like that.

You can do wavy-line quilting several times through the letters, making sure you stitch down all the ends and curves, and then follow some of the print motifs in the remaining fabrics to quilt the other patches. Anything works here.

Cheers!

"Here's to you" for accomplishing a goal – getting the well-deserved promotion, earning a degree, writing the book, opening that new business, losing the weight, running the marathon, becoming a grandmother! All great lifetime events, and each one merits a unique postcard gift.

Part of the fun in creating this simple image is finding the right fabrics. White with a frosty sheen works for glass and the nuances of color in red batik translates well for the wine.

Quilt along the edge of the glass patches and free-motion quilt swirls in the wine.

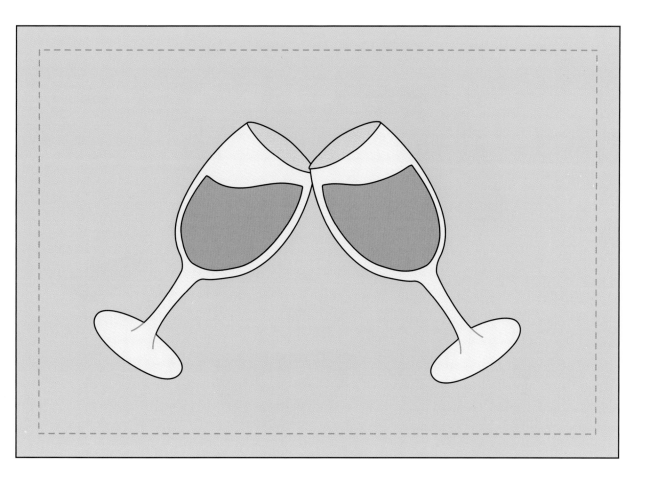

I added pearlized puffy paint to the rim and base of the glasses and then brushed the red fabrics with little bits of glitter paint in hopes of creating "glass" in front of the wine. Add ink lines with a fabric pen to extend the stems into the base.

Turn the page and choose from a variety of glasses to personalize your postcard toast. Perhaps a happy couple with contrasting beer and champagne preferences are happily celebrating their thirtieth anniversary. You can accurately commemorate that one!

CONGRATS!
WELCOME!
THANKS!
WOW!
HOORAY!

ABCDEFGHIJK
LMNOPQRSTU
VWXYZ

Party Time

A celebration with cake, lemonade and party hats says "Congratulations" for a variety of occasions including birthday, graduation, promotion and happy retirement. You might also use this as party invitations for a few special friends.

Look for a white-on-white fabric for the glass and then tints of light yellow for the lemonade and ice. Notice the straw is offset "under water."

Include a few pieces of white-fabric confetti for extra sparkle. After all patches have been fused, if the lemonade needs to be darker, follow the tip on the next page.

With monofilament thread, quilt casually around the major shapes and then in loops and swirls in the background to catch each piece of confetti at least once.

For a colorful edge treatment, use a striped fabric and cut the binding strip perpendicular to the stripes.

Color Correction

If you realize after a patch has been fused that its color is too light to show well, you can make it darker. Heat the area with a warm, dry iron and then carefully color it with a crayon in the desired shade. The heat helps the fabric absorb the colored wax.

A Little Bird Told Me

"A Little Bird Told Me" might be the way you begin your written message, the perfect way to extend congratulations for a big event – an engagement, pregnancy, adoption, promotion – or any other occasion where good wishes are in order.

As I was creating this postcard, I noticed that the flowers took on different "personalities" depending on how their blossoms and centers were tipped. Experiment with this before fusing all in place; you might find a special message in their orientations.

The garden is fine without the bird too. You might also eliminate one of the flowers for a noticeable vacancy to send an "I Miss You" message.

I got carried away with echo quilting the background, but it only needs the minimal stitching around each patch to hold all in place. Wavy horizontal lines across the entire surface, as is used in the grass, would also work well.

Needle Clean Up

If your machine needle gets sticky from the fusing product, clean it with a cotton ball dipped in alcohol.

Waiting Room

Mrs. Stork sips her tea as she waits patiently for baby's due date. Soon she'll be picking up one of the bundles and flying off to her much-anticipated destination. If the expectant parents already know the sex of the baby, include only the blue or the pink bundle. If it's twins or triplets, adjust the number of bundles and colors accordingly!

Although some details in this design have been created with thread work, you can recreate them with lines drawn with a fine-tip fabric marker, so don't let the extra stitching deter you from using this design. Those extras are shown with dashed lines in the pattern.

If you know the expected arrival date, include a calendar with that information. Trace the month and day from the templates given here before fusing the patch to the fence. You could eliminate the calendar altogether if you're not sure. Whichever way you decide to go, the parents will be delighted by your thoughtfulness.

Months and dates

JAN	MAY	SEPT
FEB	JUNE	OCT
MARCH	JULY	NOV
APRIL	AUGUST	DEC

1234567890

The Home Stretch

After designing this abstract image, I realized it needed something to tell the viewer which way is "up" because held vertically the postcard could look like some sort of landscape; hence the lettering for a title, which I like because of its triple entendre. I've made a postcard like this for two friends and waited until late in their pregnancies to send each one because of the title.

Use a delicate background print and letter it before adding the figure. If you'd like a different message, see page 61 for more words and an alphabet in this font.

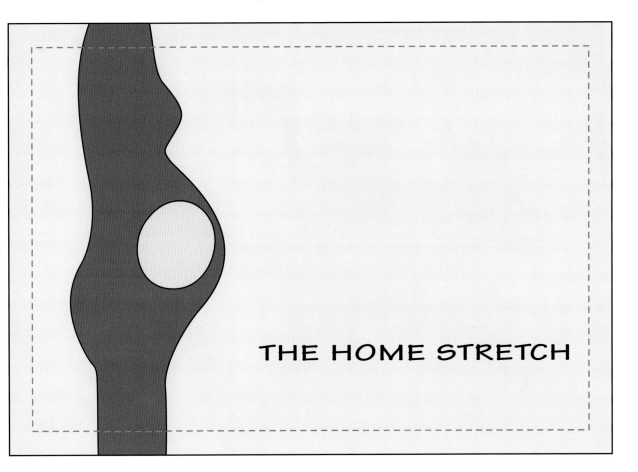

THE HOME STRETCH

I looked a long time for the perfect "baby orb" fabric and finally found what I thought worked well in a large flower print; the flower petal shading gives the oval its needed dimension.

Quilting for this simple piece is free-motion rows of horizontal waves, meandering enough to stitch down the points and curves of the patches.

Smooth Curves

When cutting out patches, move the fabric, not the scissors, as you cut. This way, you will get much smoother curves.

Animal Parade

On the following pages, you'll find a menagerie from which to choose for your postcard. One of the larger animals can lead the parade with a little guy sitting atop holding the banner and another running along side. You may have to fiddle a little to get them in position, but choose your favorites and line them up! See page 92 for another possibility.

The banner can be attached to a pole or can be held on a string around a tail, wing, or collar. For the banner, on the following pages you'll find other messages and the 50 most popular names for boys and girls. If you need to create your own words, follow the instructions on page 8 to first create a

Word Template. Trace the letters and the animals' features on the patches before fusing.

Quilt around the major shapes in the design and, if you have clouds in the sky, follow the print with a little more quilting.

Paper Peeling

If you have trouble getting a fusing paper to release for peeling from the fabric, hold the papered patch between your thumb and forefinger, paper side facing you. Score the edge of the patch with your thumbnail until it curls slightly; the paper should release along the edge.

For *Animal Parade* banner

50 most popular girls' names of 2004*

EMMA	MADELINE	ASHLEY	MORGAN
MADISON	BRIANNA	MAKAYLA	MIA
EMILY	GRACE	LILY	JASMINE
KAITLYN	ALEXIS	ANNA	ISABEL
HAILEY	SYDNEY	KAYLA	JORDAN
OLIVIA	SAMANTHA	MEGAN	RACHEL
ISABELLA	RILEY	ZOE	JULIA
HANNAH	LAUREN	MACKENZIE	JESSICA
SARAH	TAYLOR	KYLIE	SAVANNAH
ABIGAIL	CHLOE	NATALIE	ARIANA
SOPHIA	ELLA	ALLISON	VICTORIA
KAYLEE	AVA	MAYA	
ALYSSA	ELIZABETH	KATHERINE	

50 most popular boys' names of 2004*

JACOB	JACK	DANIEL	SEAN
AIDAN	JAYDEN	BENJAMIN	GABRIEL
ETHAN	LOGAN	ANTHONY	JONATHAN
RYAN	CADEN	CAMERON	SAMUEL
MATTHEW	CALEB	AUSTIN	ELIJAH
MICHAEL	ALEXANDER	EVAN	COLIN
TYLER	NATHAN	LUKE	JUSTIN
JOSHUA	NOAH	GAVIN	ALEX
NICHOLAS	WILLIAM	BRAYDEN	MASON
CONNOR	JACKSON	BRANDON	JORDAN
ZACHARY	JOSEPH	CHRISTIAN	THOMAS
ANDREW	CHRISTOPHER	JOHN	
DYLAN	JAMES	DAVID	

*According to babycenter.com

If you don't find the name you need, create a template for it by tracing from the alphabet below.

A B C D E F G H I J K L M N O P Q R S T U V W X Y Z

Additional messages for *The Home Stretch*

WELCOME!   CONGRATULATIONS!

ABCDEFGHIJKLMNOPQRSTUVWXYZ

Messages and alternative art for *Love, Love, Love* and *Luv Ya!*

BE MINE!

I LOVE YOU!

CALL ME!

KISS ME!

ABCDEFGH
IJKLMNOPQR
STUVWXYZ!

Pie & Coffee

Send your friend this little piece of art as a thank you for her lunch party, for helping you with the kids so many times, for letting you "volunteer" her for the fund-raising committee, or for just being there when you need to talk.

Your cherry pie could easily turn into blueberry or apple. Take off the top crust and make pumpkin; change to yellow filling and add mounds of white for lemon meringue or coconut custard – whatever's her favorite.

Part of the fun in a design like this is looking through your fabric stash to create the perfect pie and the coffee mug. Find a lightly patterned white for the steam; pay attention to the "left overs" as you cut the swirls out – the negative areas make more usable swirls.

For quilting, stitch down the edges of the patches with monofilament thread. If you feel creative, add more quilted swirls of steam in the background.

Wine & Cheese

om and Jenny invited my husband and me, and daughter Alissa with her family, to spend Christmas in their extraordinary mountain home while they were out of town. This way, we could be "right down the road" from daughter Maria and her family. What a treat that was for all of us. As part of our thank you, I made and sent a postcard in this design to our absentee hosts, choosing colors and prints to complement their decor. The framed card now hangs in their kitchen.

Can you tell the surface of the wine is a lighter yellow than the wine below? The contrast of these two yellows was not great enough so I added tiny

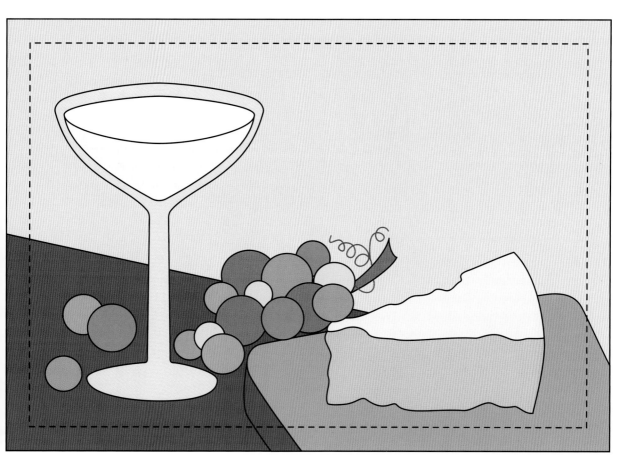

dots of brown permanent ink where they meet, which also defines the front rim of the glass. Stitching with gold or tan thread would create a similar effect.

Add the vine tendrils with black or dark brown permanent ink after all the patches are in place.

Quilting in the background follows the print motif, but any random free-motion quilting will be fine. I outline stitched the grapes and glass, quilted swirls in the wine, and circles in the cheese.

Bouquet

This delicate bouquet adapts easily to any seasonal palette. Gather fabrics in the color collection you want, making sure each one has enough contrast to the background fabric. Include a few darker shades and a few brights to add a little drama. Follow the pattern or just cut out lots of blossoms and leaves and create your own arrangement.

After all the patches were fused, I noticed that the vase didn't stand out quite enough, so I quilted a line of stitches with gray thread just outside the patch.

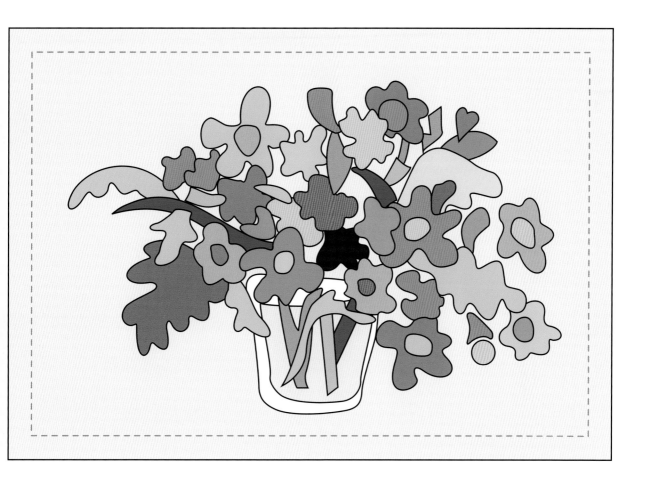

Casually outline the flowers and leaves, stems, water and vase with free-motion quilting.

You may want to make several of this design as it works well for "Happy Mother's Day," "Happy Birthday," " Get Well, " "Thank You" and "I'm Thinking of You."

If you prefer a simpler bouquet, use fewer large flowers from *Whimsy Garden* on the following page and make a "ceramic" vase with print fabric (see page 92).

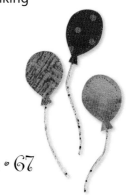

Any Occasion ◦ 67

Whimsy Garden

 ind a green print with a "wash" of lights and darks for a lively background, and then fill your garden with bright flowers and curving leaves. You may not need the placement guide for this pattern; put the blossoms wherever you like. No two gardens are the same and yours can grow just the way you want it.

Quilting on this postcard is mostly a surface design of loops and twirls to catch points and little sections in the stitching.

Notice how the red binding brings out the red swirls and center patches in the flowers? Because red is green's complement, the background looks more vivid too.

Saving Snippets

As you make more postcards, you'll be glad to have fused fabrics to work with later. Designate a container for little snippets — plastic food containers are ideal — and cut out patches over it. Let the little pieces fall into the container.

The Open Door

At first, I was hesitant about including this design, but the more I thought about the possibilities, the more interesting it became. You could use this image to celebrate passage from one life event to another. A print of a seascape or mountains through the doorway would work for "Happy Retirement" or "Bon Voyage." A city skyline print might be appropriate for "Happy Graduation," "Our Best for Your New Adventure" or "Good Luck."

The postcard on page 92 uses a baby-talk print through an interior doorway to the nursery – your perfect "Congratulations" gift for friends who have just become parents.

Choose fabric that looks like wallpaper as the background. How about a shiny button for the doorknob instead of a patch? And rather than the potted plant, add flowers from *Bouquet* on page 66 to the large container.

Quilt around the major shapes in this design with mono-filament thread.

Window Work

To help identify which area of a print will work best for a patch, first cut a hole in a piece of heavy paper the shape of that patch. Move the paper "window" across the print until you like the composition. Trace the edge of the opening on the fabric with a chalk pencil and cut on this line.

Playmates

You'll probably want to adjust the boy/girl combination to fit your purpose for this postcard. I used fabrics to reflect three children of different personalities, but your choices also might portray different cultures with ethnic prints.

The balloon strings were slivers of fuse-backed fabric that I curved just in front of the hot iron as I pressed them in place. Zigzagging across pearl cotton or thin string with monofilament thread would work just as well. Perhaps add some ribbon bows at the necks of the balloons for added dimension.

This design would be fun to send for a kindergarten graduation, a thank you for a fun play date or a party invitation to a few special little guests.

Quilt a Wave

When quilting a thin patch or a patch with straight edges, quilt a wavy line from side to side. This will hold down the patch and avoid splitting threads along the edges. See the strings of the balloons on this card.

Hey, Girlfriend!

Celebrate shopping time with your girlfriend with this whimsical post-card. Choose a light print for both figures, or use different prints that reflect two distinct personalities. Adjust the clothes if you like – shorts, straight skirt, longer pants – and hairdos too. How about adorning the ladies with red hats to celebrate their fifty-and-beyond stature in life?

Quilt around the major shapes with monofilament thread.

Although most of the designs in this book have little or no embellishment, this one seemed perfect for a little glitz. Rhinestones, tiny buttons, ribbon,

braid, little silk flowers, rickrack, feathers or sequins can be glued on to accessorize. Or use puff paints to draw jewelry and trims.

Fusing Caution

Pay close attention to the fusing time. If you fuse too long, the fabric might scorch, the fabric may absorb the webbing and become ineffective, or the fabric color under a patch may show through too much.

Floating Leaves

Work on a dark background with medium to bright print patches for this graphic design. I especially like batik prints because the fabric doesn't ravel along all these curved edges and many prints are appropriate for leaf shapes. When layering patches, make sure the values of the colors contrast enough so you enjoy each motif.

After fusing all the patches in place, I was hesitant to quilt them because I liked the flat, distinct shapes just the way they were. However, with clear monofilament thread, I free-motion quilted veins in all the leaves to give them texture. The quilting does add another dimension to the design that you can appreciate close up, but this image works particularly well

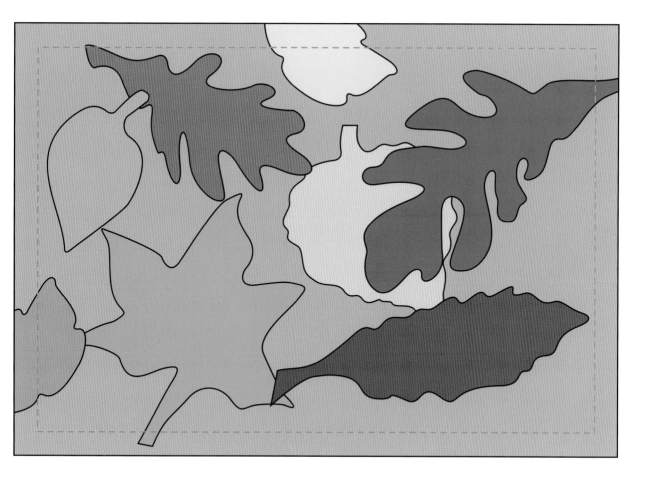

that you can appreciate close up, but this image works particularly well as a no-sew postcard.

If you want a design specific to the vegetation in your locale, or if you'd like to make an original design with more variety in leaf sizes, look on the following pages for patterns. Also, see the *Floating Leaves* variation on page 92; start with a basic pattern and change it a little as you cut each subsequent patch to get the unique shapes.

The Road Ahead

hildlike prints, bright colors and the dancing attitude of the trees make this a carefree landscape. Notice that the distant hill and road are lighter tints of the foreground green and yellow to create a feeling of depth. I fused white fabric to the back of the bright yellow so the dark green wouldn't show through when the road was fused in place.

For a more serene look, try the patches in naturalistic fabrics – leaf prints for the trees, grass prints for the hills, pebbly prints for the road.

Quilt the road and hills with wavy lines and outline quilt the trees, adding a few loops inside the larger ones.

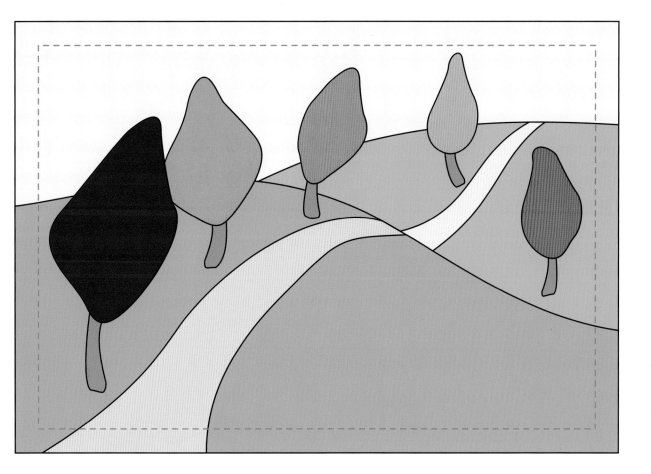

This design could work for messages of "Congratulations on your Graduation," "Bon Voyage," "I'll Miss You" and "Happy Retirement," whether interpreted with whimsical or more naturalistic fabrics.

Change for the Better

If you're not happy with a particular patch after it's been fused in place, reheat it with a warm iron and peel it off. The patch probably has enough fusible web to be repositioned at least once more.

By the Sea

Having lived all my life in beautiful but land-locked Colorado, I dream about having a cottage by the sea. Big enough for all the family, it's on a secluded beach with white sand and flowering dunes – like the one I've pictured here. The cottage is off to the right just out of the picture. But wait, do flowers bloom on dunes or is this just in my fantasy?

The challenge for this design is finding the perfect sea fabric. I like this batik with its washes of teal and periwinkle, which give depth to the water.

Since this design doesn't really have a background patch, start with a 4½" x 6½" piece of muslin. Cut sky and sand fabrics each at 2¼" x 6½"

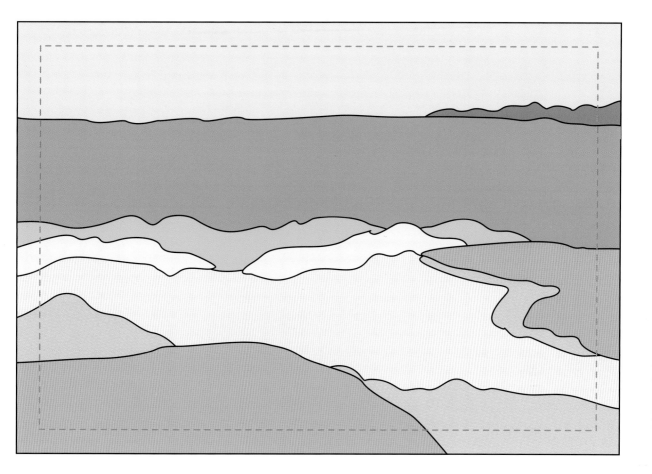

and lightly fuse them to
the muslin. Then add the
remaining patches.

Outline quilt the distant
land form, the waves,
rocks and the dunes.
Quilt wavy lines in the
sea and then tiny loops
 in the sand for a
pebbly texture.

Steaming the Stiffener

If your piece of stiffener has kept
its curve from being wrapped
around the bolt, hover over it
with a hot steam iron for a few
moments. It should flatten nicely.

Mountain Vista

For twenty years, we lived in the Colorado mountains. This scene reminds me of Strawberry Trail where, every September, we cut wood to burn as our primary heat source during the winter.

Gather several white prints that remind you of aspen or birch tree bark, or draw your own bark pattern with black ink on white or gray fabric. Then find a grayed green and a brighter green for the meadow, dark blue for close mountains and a purple for the distant ones. On the sky background, fuse the purple, blue and then the greens to it. Position and fuse one group of trees and then complete with the remaining group.

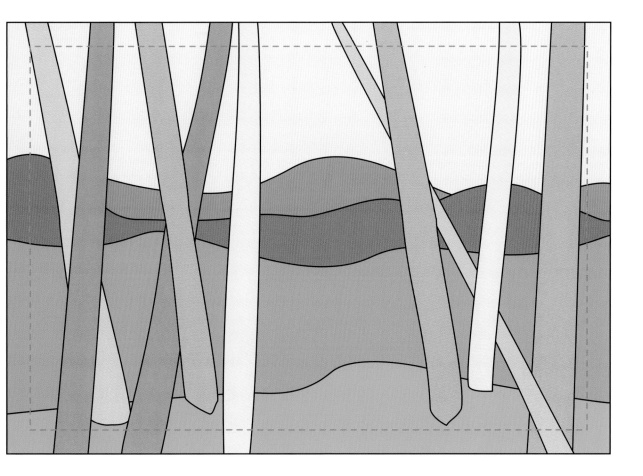

Quilting follows the edge of the patches, with some zigzags in along the tree trunks to give them texture.

I especially like the way the mottled batik binding fabric on this card echoes the greens, blue and purple of the scene.

Because of its scenic character, this quilt could be a gift for most any occasion; if you send it for a birthday, you could add a little cake on the address side. See the pattern on page 11.

Close to the Forest

Inspiration for this pattern came from the the tree trunks of *Mountain Vista*, page 84. I wanted an abstract design with a masculine character that could also feature beautiful fabrics. A variety of values and print sizes create texture and depth.

The strips are quilted in a random wavy pattern along each edge; this works better than a straight stitch which tends to split the threads and encourage fraying. Since most of the fabrics are dark, I used a smoky monofilament thread in the top and black in the bobbin.

Like the other abstract or geo-

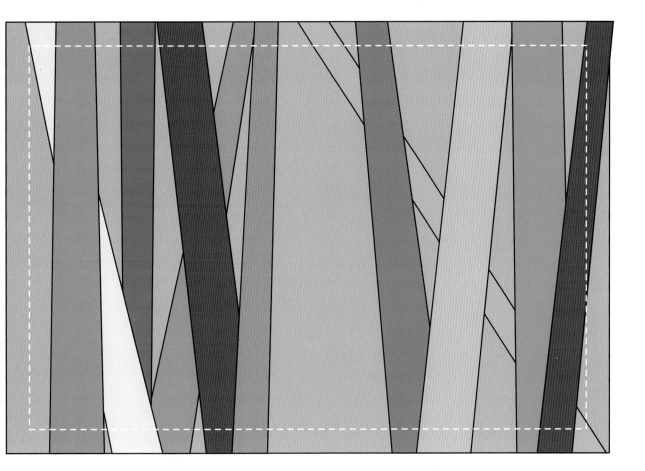

Like the other abstract or geo-
metric designs in this book, this
one will work well for a variety
of purposes. And with fabrics in
different styles – hearts and
flowers, primary colors, animal
prints, reproduction prints – it's
adaptable to a wide range of
ages and personalities.

Dots and Dashes

To better define the shape of
a patch, add a fine line of dots –
or just a fine line – on the background just outside the patch. See
the mug in Pie & Coffee,
page 62; it shows up
better with the line.

Lattice

This design is fun to create after you've developed a stash of fuse-backed fabrics so you don't have to prepare a bunch of little strips.

I wanted this to look like sun shining through lattice. A rule I made for myself was to use cool colored fabrics in one direction and warm colored fabrics in the other.

Start with a 5"x 7" background (larger than the finished size). Follow the pattern or just cut strips in random widths and no longer than 8". Arrange all the strips needed for one direction on the background fabric. To stabilize them for weaving, fuse these strips down only ⅛"

in along the top and one side edge of the background patch. Weave the remaining strips in and out to create the lattice look. Fuse all down and then trim the piece to 4½" x 6½".

Quilt wavy lines through the center of each of the strips.

For a variation, use pastel or neutral prints for the strips and then add a heart, flower, leaf or animal from another pattern in this book. This versatile design will work well for any occasion as a nice little piece of art for your message on the back.

Tileworks

Y ou might find that this is your favorite design because it can do so much with so little work. With the one tile turned, your message can be "To My Special Friend." Straighten it out and arrange colors in a gradation for a sunrise effect and the message becomes "Have a Great Day." Replace the tiles with some of the little motifs patterned here and make gardens or kisses and hugs or mountain scenes. Leave one place on the grid empty and the message becomes "I Miss You."

Any quilting scheme is good that stitches down points and tiny elements of the motifs. Try loops and swirls or wavy lines than meander enough to catch every patch.

Turn to page 92 to find a patriotic variation of this postcard design.

Variations

From Tileworks,
page 90

From Bouquet and Whimsy Garden,
pages 66 & 68

From The Open Door, page 70

From Floating Leaves, page 76

From Animal Parade, page 56

From Love, Love, Love, page 38

Combinations

From the silhouette option in Star Party, page 23, and waves, beach and dunes in By the Sea, page 82

From Mountain Vista, page 84 and trees and hill from The Road Ahead, page 80

From lettering in Congrats!, page 42; figure in Playmates, page 72; and flowers in Bouquet, page 66 and Valentine Tree, page 36

THANK YOU!

Other Ideas

A speedy way to create an image for a postcard is to cut out and fuse a motif from a printed fabric onto a background patch. Both the teapot and the frog postcards were done in this "broderie perse" style and finished with fused binding.

And, here's a great home for those orphaned UFO blocks (UnFinished Objects). Cut 4½" x 6½" sections and use them as the surface designs for postcards to mail to your favorite quilt-loving friends.

Whole Cloth

Select a print that has distinct images. Quilt around these images and sew on a binding. Or for a 20-minute project, sandwich the stiffener between the print and the backing and then finish with a fused binding!

Message Ideas to Trace

Birthday

Wishing you a year of joy and love.

Wishing you a year of dreams come true.

A very special birthday wish to my very special friend.

Enjoy the pleasures of the day.

Friendship

I'm glad you're my friend.

Thanks for being there.

Of all my gifts, you are my favorite.

Forgive me.

Thank you for being so kind.

Congratulations

May everything wonderful come your way.

Enjoy! You deserve it.

The best is yet to come.

Here's to you.

Thinking of you and all the happy days ahead.

New Baby

To a New Little Star

Welcome Little One

Get Well

Sending love and get well wishes.

May each day get better and brighter.